RADICAL GOD talk

Devotional | Interactive | Journal

MONICA WITHERS

I dedicate this book to the Holy Spirit. How can
I thank YOU for allowing me to be your vessel?
And I dedicate this book to my most wonderful
partner and husband, Mark Withers.
You are always my biggest fan.

ACKNOWLEDGEMENTS

Special thanks to Nicole Mountz, Kali Ritchey, Christy Kaneta and Laurie Kaneta for sharing
their brains, their hearts and their creativity in the development of this book. You girls rock!
Thanks to my editor, Kaye. With your encouragement, this book took on a whole new life.
And thanks to Garry Townsley, who went way out of the box to design this book.

STUFF in the book

God talk...how & why

Hey Girl~

Throughout these pages God will be talking to you. I'm sure of it. And I want to tell you how I know.

I was born again in my 30s, and almost immediately I began to sense a calling to write from the Spirit of God. It was almost an irresistible urge. This was a huge surprise to me and to all those who knew me because I had struggled all the way through school and had the grades to prove it. I never liked writing. Even texting was way too many words for me. I knew only heaven could inspire me this way.

In fact, something supernatural began to take place. From a place of communion with the Lord, words began to pour from my heart to the page. In the beginning, I wrote just one word at a time - whatever word I heard the Holy Spirit speak to my heart. As the years progressed, the process of writing became easier and the words flowed with greater unction.

I learned the pen was in my hand, but the message came from His heart.

Now the time has come to share God Talk with you.

Because, girlfriend, God is talking to you.

But this is a different kind of journal.

This is a journal where you interact with God. This is a journey to take one day at a time and to allow HIS Word to transform you into the wonderful, beautiful and talented person HE has called you to be.

Each day you will listen, write, declare and walk out all God has intended you to be. It's a fellowship with the Father. It's an intimate walk with HIM, and in this process, you will see yourself in a new and different way. You will begin to see yourself become bold and strong. You will begin to see yourself become the person God intends you to be.

Some days you will wait quietly with HIM, or maybe you will write out what HE is saying to you. Maybe you will speak and declare who HE says you are, or maybe you will just enjoy HIS glorious presence. Whatever HE speaks to your heart, jump in with both feet. Raise your hands! Shout to the Lord! And just be you!

I pray this journal will take you to a deeper place with Jesus so that you may walk the path HE has laid before you with boldness, confidence and the knowledge of who you are in Him. Be blessed!

Monica

▶ WARNING:

During the reading of this book your life might be radically changed. You might see things in a new way. You might get a new take on life. You might get a new take on yourself.

You might get the point.

Real life that's really worth living
is all about **JESUS.**

So read this book with your head **AND** your heart, and take it to heart.

You may be asked to do things you question.
You may be asked to do things that sound crazy.
But...
GO with it!
DO what the page says!
GO ahead. Let change happen. You may begin to live more radically and really, really like it.

INSTRUCTION #1

first things first.

To have real GOD TALK, you gotta know GOD.

Have you ever made Jesus Christ your Lord and Savior? If you say no or you don't know, let's take care of that right now.

You can't understand your life or life at all until you get the Author of Life inside.

Praying this prayer is quick. It's easy. And it's the best decision you'll ever make. Simply pray these words from your heart aloud:

Father, in the name of Jesus, I come to you today to receive Jesus as my Lord and Savior. Your Word says if we confess with our mouth and believe with our hearts that Jesus died and was raised from the dead, we will be saved. Your Word also says if we confess our sins, You are faithful and just to forgive us of all unrighteousness.
So today I receive You into my heart. I make You the Lord of my life. I surrender to Your will.

Because of You...
I am the righteousness of God thru Christ.
I am forgiven.
I am more than a conquer in Christ Jesus.
I am worthy, holy, pure and without blame before You.
I have the same Spirit in me as Jesus has in Him, and I have all the authority He has given me in the name of Jesus.

brace yourself.

STAND HERE

(Maybe you'll want to wipe your feet first.)

NOW DECLARE: I'm willing to rip open my thinking and let God in. I want an invasion of God in my life because I'm serious about living a new way. Holy Ghost, open my mind and fill my heart with God. Help me follow the steps of life that You've already planned for me.

INSTRUCTION #3.

READ!

HOW ELSE ARE YOU GOING TO GET IT DONE? YOU'VE GOT TO START SOMEWHERE.

SCRIBBLE WILDLY AND VIOLENTLY WITH RECKLESS ABANDON.

This scribble is your story without God in it. Let God be your guide. Let Him help you write your story.

LET'S BE CLEAR HERE. THERE ARE NO RULES.

Take off your religious robes and your doctrinal ways. Forget what everyone else says. Now listen to what God says.

So What's your story?

Your story has already been told. It's already written in The Book of Life.

Now all you need to do is walk it out, step by step, faith on faith and watch it come alive!

Your life is a love story, a story of Me wooing you in and showering you with My love.

The world feels like it needs gadgets and toys to feel good, but one touch of My hand and your heart will melt and your stormy emotions will subside.

Then you will know deep in your heart who I've created you to be and what's on the inside.

So let your story be told one chapter at a time, and watch your life unfold before your very eyes.

Revelation 3:5 (NIV) The one who is victorious will, like them, be dressed in white. I will never blot out the name of that person from the book of life, but will acknowledge that name before my Father and his angels.

J _____

E _____

S _____

U _____

S _____

Only just begun

No eye has seen. No ear has heard.

No mind can conceive what God has planned for those who love him.

When you look out what do you see? Although you feel lost and afraid, remember you're never alone. You'll never have to walk without ME beside you encouraging you along.

MY child, this world may seem dark, unfriendly and cruel but also enticing and full of fun. Neither are of ME, and neither will lead you to joy, peace and the abundance of ME.

Remember, no eye has seen the true glory of the Lord.

No ear has heard the far away cry, and no man can conceive the dreams, the unseen I have prepared for each one.

But when you seek ME, seek heavenly things. Then you can see and conceive what I have done. Remember, I give you a life full and abundant, but you must grab hold and receive steps one by one.

By faith you will have, ask, and it will be done.

Your life has only just begun and the journey you've started cannot compare to the places you are about to enter on. Don't be afraid or draw back, for the road ahead has great and marvelous views and lives to be touched.

So don't look at the things of this world. Look unto ME, Jesus, the One, the True, the One who has called you.

1 Corinthians 2:9 (NLT)

...No eye has seen, no ear has heard, and no mind has imagined what God has prepared for those who love him.

Who is God anyway?

BIKES, SKATEBOARDS AND SUCH.
COMPUTERS, PHONE AND IPAD YOU SAY.
I CAN'T LIVE IN THIS WORLD WITHOUT THESE;. WHAT WOULD THEY SAY?

It's a new time, a new way, who is this God anyway?

He seems so far, far away. Nothing is impossible for me.
If I study really hard, I can do anything.
Who cares who I hurt? It's all about me and what I can do to succeed.
People don't count unless they are with me.
Success, money and all. Oh, I can't live without it or else I'll fall.
My life is my own. It's all about me. I'm #1.

MY child, is that what you believe? That life is only about you? But did you know I died even for you?

It's not your own life when you give it away, when you say yes to ME. It's a lifetime of change.

Your life is no longer your own, but the impossibilities are way above what you could ever know.

You think I'm too far away? I AM only a word spoken, a small breath away.

You believe in selfish gain? But when you lay it all down, then will you win the mighty crown.

Success is all you want? But with ME you will succeed beyond all you ever thought.

So come to ME and check ME out.

Come and allow ME to show you what I'm all about.

What a difference you'll make in the lives all around, but you will have to lay your own life down.

Take up your cross, and boy, what you will see.

MY glory, MY love and a new heart and new eyes to see.

GALATIANS 2:20

I have been crucified with Christ; it is no longer I who live, but Christ lives in me; and the life which I now live in the flesh I live by faith in the Son of God, who loved me and gave Himself for me.

Do I have a purpose? Does God have a plan for me? Where am I going? What has God called me to do? Will I succeed? Will I crash and burn?

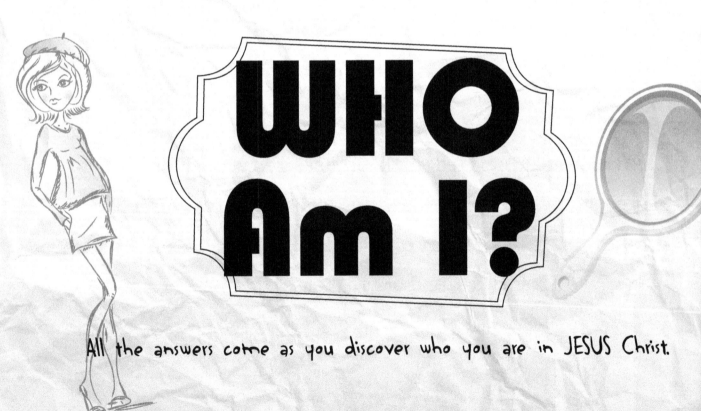

WHO Am I?

All the answers come as you discover who you are in JESUS Christ.

CHRIST LIVES IN ME

Write it Out!

_____

_____

_____

_____

_____

_____

_____

_____

_____

_____

pretend your life is a twitter feed.

who or what can you **UNFOLLOW?**

Don't be a follower

It is not MY best when you follow your own plan. It's not always the way I have intended for you to go. Do not be a follower of those around you, but step aside and let ME show you the way.

Do not follow the ways of this world, but allow ME to guide you.

There may be a hurting heart somewhere along the way, but when you listen to those all around, you miss what I have to say. Then you can be led astray.

My will for you is to grow, flourish and mature in the knowledge of who I AM

For when you follow ME, then you can lead those to a new place and know MY great and mighty plan.

So let MY Word, MY hand and MY Spirit lead you. Then you will be strong and fit, and then you will know MY best. I will show you the right way.

Psalm 25:4-5 (The Message)

Show me how you work, GOD; School me in your ways.
Take me by the hand; Lead me down the path of truth.
You are my Savior, aren't you?

WHAT'S LOVE GOT TO DO WITH IT?

LOVE is a funny thing. It's an emotion that comes and goes. It's a feeling you cannot control. Yet...

MY LOVE is everlasting.

MY LOVE is unconditional.

MY LOVE doesn't fade in and out.

When you allow ME to LOVE you, all else fades away. Everything subsides, and you know you are safe. Allow ME to pour over you, MY GREAT LOVE. Allow ME to fill you full and LOVE you like you've never been LOVED before.

MY LOVE will never fail you. MY LOVE will never lead you astray. And no matter what you do or what you say, I will always LOVE you. MY LOVE is here to stay.

1 John 4:16 (NLT)
We know how much God loves us, and we have put our trust in his love. God is love, and all who live in love live in God, and God lives in them.

Jeremiah 31:3 (NIV)
The LORD appeared to us in the past, saying: "I have loved you with an everlasting love; I have drawn you with unfailing-kindness."

LOVE.

Think on this.

If I give everything I own to the poor and even go to the stake to be burned as a martyr, but I don' t love, I' ve gotten nowhere.

So, no matter what I say, what I believe, and what I do, I'm bankrupt without love.

Love never gives up.

Love cares more for others than for self.

Love doesn't want what it doesn't have.

Love doesn't strut,

Doesn't have a swelled head,

Doesn't force itself on others,

Isn't always "me first,"

Doesn't fly off the handle,

Doesn't keep score of the sins of others,

Doesn't revel when others grovel,

Takes pleasure in the flowering of truth,

Puts up with anything,

Trusts God always,

Always looks for the best,

Never looks back,

But keeps going to the end.

Love never dies.

Taken from The Message.

1 Corinthians 13: 3-8

We sit with Jesus in heavenly places.

EPH. 2:6

Get perspective. Climb up high. Then imagine this. The closer you get to God, the bigger you dream and the smaller your problems. Look around up there. Get used to being on top of things.

THE BIG PICTURE

Have you ever thought about the big picture in life?

Have you ever asked ME, "God, what are You calling me to be?"

I do have great plans. I do have a place for you to go. I have called you for ME.

Sometimes life's issues are overwhelming. It may seem like the world is coming to an end. This is the time to run into MY arms. This is the time to come to that quiet, secret place and rest in ME. I will speak words of comfort, peace and breathe life into you.

Don't get caught up in all the worldly issues and noise, but come to ME and trust I will show you where and when you need to go.

Come to ME, and ask and hear ME say, "MY child, I AM all you will ever need. So come and ask and follow ME."

Jeremiah 33:3 (The Message)

"Call to me and I will answer you. I'll tell you marvelous and wondrous things that you could never figure out on your own."

James 4:3-4

You ask and do not receive, because you ask amiss, that you may spend it on your pleasures.

Write it Out!

_____

_____

_____

_____

_____

_____

_____

_____

_____

_____

Bells & Whistles

Bells and whistles, social media and all.
If only you would listen to Me as you much as you do to it all.

Let your attention be drawn to what really counts. Let your heart be filled with things from above instead of those things from which you think you can't live without.

Oh, MY precious child, if you would only see.
MY love, MY goodness and the glory surrounding ME.

Take a quick glance. Take a moment to see, for what you're going after is not at all what I meant for you to be.

· · · · ·

1 John 2:15-17 (The Message)

Don't love the world's ways. Don't love the world's goods. Love of the world squeezes out love for the Father. Practically everything that goes on in the world—wanting your own way, wanting everything for yourself, wanting to appear important—has nothing to do with the Father. It just isolates you from him. The world and all its wanting, wanting, wanting is on the way out—but whoever does what God wants is set for eternity.

GO some-where without your phone today. TALK WITH GOD

Sit quiet with Him.

Imagine this is God's plan for you. Look up scriptures about what God has in store for you and write them in your stepping stones.

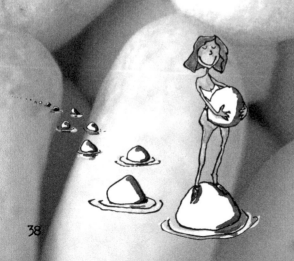

Check out these scriptures:
Jeremiah 29:11
Isaiah 43:1 and John 15:16
Psalm 32:8 and Psalm 119:105

Just stop!

MY beloved child, the very one I adore.

Listen for a moment. Listen with a heart open and ready to receive.

Listen even if you don't believe.

~~STOP.~~ Take a few minutes, and ask ME before you choose. Let ME show you an even better way, for I will take you places only I can go.

~~STOP.~~ Be still and listen to ME for the steps I have placed before you will lead you to ME and then is when you will know how to succeed.

~~STOP.~~ Take a moment and listen to ME.

~~~~~~~~~~~~~~~~~~~~~~~~~~~~~~

Psalm 37:23-24 (The Message)

Stalwart walks in step with God; his path blazed by God, he's happy.
If he stumbles, he's not down for long; God has a grip on his hand.

CHEW ON THIS!

*WARNING:
DO NOT
SWALLOW
PAPER

stop listening!

YOU are MY redeemed. You are worthy and pure before ME. You are the apple of MY eye.

Don't listen to the ones who say otherwise. Don't be afraid to walk away when they speak like fools. Allow ME to fill you full.

It's a scary world. It's a place of deceit, lies and false accusations. But if you come before ME, I will show you who I have created you to be.

For what the world sees and knows is but a flashy sign here today and gone tomorrow. But I will not leave you behind. I will not turn MY back on you. You are the one I have placed MY holy hand upon.

Come to our quiet place and lay it all down. Talk with ME, and let ME show you who I have made you to be. You are worthy, pure. You are MY redeemed.

Psalm 17:8 (NIV)

Keep me as the apple of your eye;
hide me in the shadow of your wings.

Write it Out!

_____

_____

_____

_____

_____

_____

_____

_____

_____

_____

_____

Just Say what I say!

I **can** do all things thru Christ!
God is GREAT in me!

God is 4 Me!

GOD ALWAYS CAUSES ME TO TRIUMPH!

Curve ball

IN times of trials and chaos, remember I AM right beside you leading you on.

MY hand is holding you close and giving you all the insight and direction you need to move forward unharmed, steady and strong.

But you must learn to follow ME and follow MY lead even when times get rough. I will not let you fall or fumble. I will keep you upright, strong and tough.

Come to ME in these times and rest in MY arms. Be who I've made you to be.

Child of MINE, you are strong, courageous and full of My power, but you must learn to tap in to Me and believe.

When life throws you balls you cannot return, believe I have you exactly where I need you to be.

Stay close. Stay in faith. And put all your trust in ME, for I AM your loving Father, your Savior, I AM HE.

John 16:33 (AMP)

I have told you these things, so that in Me you may have [perfect] peace and confidence. In the world you have tribulation and trials and distress and frustration; but be of good cheer [take courage; be confident, certain, undaunted]! For I have overcome the world. [I have deprived it of power to harm you and have conquered it for you.]

James 1:2-4 (The Message)

Consider it a sheer gift, friends, when tests and challenges come at you from all sides. You know that under pressure, your faith-life is forced into the open and shows its true colors. So don't try to get out of anything prematurely. Let it do its work so you become mature and well-developed, not deficient in any way.

BURN BABY BURN

Let the fire within kindle hotter and hotter.

Let that desire I have placed deep down inside continue to burn and continue to grow until it's ready to explode.

Many have great dreams, visions and big promises, but they feel pushed down. Many feel the flame has died out.

But I AM saying that flicker will continue to ignite and will continue to burn and grow in MY sight.

I will open doors.

I will make a way where there seemed no way.

I will make the steps for MY righteous. I will delight MYSELF in you, and I will make it plain and clear to see all that's in front of you.

So let the fire burn within. Be excited about that which once was out and smoldering, but is now lit and ready to ignite.

Let the fire burn within!

Ezekiel 20:47-48 (The Message)

'Listen to the Message of God! God, the Master, says, I'll set a fire in you that will burn up every tree, dead trees and live trees alike. Nobody will put out the fire. The whole country from south to north will be blackened by it. Everyone is going to see that I, God, started the fire and that it's not going to be put out.'

Take time to just pray...
What's the vision burning inside?

If there isnt anything, ask God to ignite one!

Write it Out!

_____

_____

_____

_____

_____

_____

_____

_____

_____

_____

_____

stop the chatter and listen

Child, why are you downcast and afraid?

Why do you allow the voice of the enemy to fill your mind with negative thoughts and lies of who you should be?

Listen to ME! Stop all the chatter. Stop all the noise. And believe in ME.

MY words are comfort, peace and joy.

MY words will encourage and build you up to overflow your heart with all that is good. Don't allow circumstances and the ways of this world to pull you down, but look up and see MY goodness and glory all around.

Take time to be with ME, and I will show you great and mighty things, ways to dream big and greater thoughts of who I have called you to be.

So don't be downcast or afraid, but come and be close beside ME. Hear the Word of the Lord say that you are called, chosen and free.

You are MY daughter, the redeemed.

Psalm 42:11 (AMP)

Why are you cast down, O my inner self? And why should you moan over me and be disquieted within me? Hope in God and wait expectantly for Him, for I shall yet praise Him, Who is the help of my countenance, and my God.

Lies you tell yourself	What God says!
I am alone	God will never leave me (Heb. 13:5). I won't fear. HE'S with me (Is. 41:10).
I'm so stupid	I have the mind of Christ (1 Cor. 2:16). I have anointing and know all things (1 Jn. 2:20).
I'm ugly	I am fearfully and wonderfully made (Ps. 139:14).
I'm unworthy	God chose me (Eph. 1:4). I'm chosen, royal, holy and special (1Pet. 2:9).
I can't	I can do all things through Christ (Phil. 4:13). I am more than a conqueror (Ro. 8:37).
I've made too many mistakes	I'm redeemed through HIS blood (Eph. 1:7). Jesus delivered me out of darkness into light (Col. 1:13). HE forgives all my sin (1Jn. 1:9).
I am sick	By HIS stripes I am healed (1Pet. 2:24, Is. 53:4). HE healed them all (Mt. 4:24).
I am unloved	HE loved me first (1Jn. 4:10). I abide in His love (John 15:9). Nothing! shall separate me from HIS love (Ro. 8:38-39).
I am poor	HE will meet all my needs (Phil. 4:19). As I give it will be given back to me (Lk. 6:38).
I don't have any real plans in life	God has big plans for me (Jer. 29:11). I am HIS workmanship (Eph. 2:10). I am confident HE will complete the good work HE began in me (Phil. 1:6).

Write more lies you hear on the left.   Write more of what God says on the right.

Read Ephesians 1:4 in The Amplified Bible, and write out words of affirmation about yourself.

WHOSE APPROVAL Я U LOOKING 4?

DO you really believe?

Do you say with your mouth but not believe in your heart?
When you truly believe with your whole heart, only then will things change. Only then will your life transform.

You look to others for confirmation. Sometimes you want their approval more than you want MINE. When this happens, you lose focus of who I have created you to be; you lose focus of ME.

Don't allow your surroundings to determine what you believe.

Don't always believe what you see. All you see is only temporal while MY unseen is eternal.

Don't allow your emotions to predict which way you will turn. Come to ME and hear that still small voice encourage you and help you along.

It's from your heart that you truly believe, so spend more time quietly on your knees as your heart and mind transform to the image of ME.

Romans 10:10 (AMP)

For with the heart a person believes (adheres to, trusts in, and relies on Christ) and so is justified (declared righteous, acceptable to God), and with the mouth he confesses (declares openly and speaks out freely his faith) and confirms [his] salvation.

2 Corinthians 4:18

While we do not look at the things which are seen, but at the things which are not seen. For the things which are seen are temporary, but the things which are not seen are eternal.

Write it Out!

_____

_____

_____

_____

_____

_____

_____

_____

_____

_____

There's no better way

Some days you awake rejoicing in ME. Some days you awake downcast and afraid.

Why?

Don't you know that I live on the inside? I AM here every morning waiting for your smile, your reply.

Every day is a good day, a day to rejoice and enjoy.

Refuse to allow feelings and circumstances to dictate your attitude for the day. Instead, be led by MY Spirit. Let your heart be filled with MY love, goodness and joy, and watch your life transform.

Watch and enjoy the details of the day.

Live your life greatly delighted in Me. There's no better way.

Philippians 4:4-5 (The Message)

Celebrate God all day, every day. I mean, revel in him! Make it as clear as you can to all you meet that you're on their side, working with them and not against them. Help them see that the Master is about to arrive. He could show up any minute!

Romans 8:14 (NIV)

For those who are led by the Spirit of God are the children of God.

Psalm 37:3-4 (The Message)

Get insurance with GOD and do a good deed, settle down and stick to your last.
Keep company with GOD, get in on the best.

CRANK
up some music
really **LOUD!**
praise! clap!
shout! jump!
All to God!

Trace your hand on this page with a brightly colored marker. On each finger write a word that describes how God sees you. Add jewelry and nail color! God sure didn't forget to decorate you.

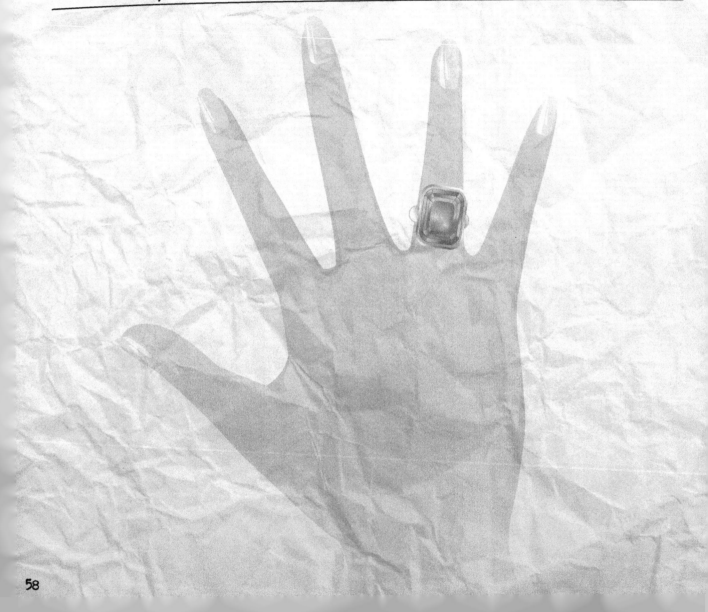

DON'T COMPARE

MY child, no matter how hard life may seem, believe I have you in the palm of MY hand. If you look up and talk to ME, I will guide you along the path of life set before you.

Don't compare yourself to those around.

I have made you unique and beautiful.

You're YOU.

Do not allow the outside influences or the people all around to tell you who you are or who they think you're supposed to be.

Just be you. Be who I have created you to be--strong, faithful, anointed and free.

You're a child of the Most High God, a light for the world to see.

Always remember you are in the palm of MY hand, and you are who I have said you would be.

Don't look back. Just come and follow ME and then you will see the path lit beneath your feet.

- -

Isaiah 49:16

See, I have inscribed you on the palm of My hands....

Matthew 5:16

Let your light so shine before men, that they may see your good works and glorify your Father in heaven.

SO LONG TEMPTATION

Sayonara. Bye bye. Ciao. Hasta la vista, baby. Don t let the door hit you on the way out!

1, Get a blank piece of paper.
2. Write down your greatest temptations. Be honest.
3. Over the SINK, strike a match.
4. Watch your temptations burn.
5. Ask the Holy Ghost to burn up those desires in you.

Everyone is doing it

THE sounds, the smells, the clatter of this world.

Oh how enticing it can be. The temptation is sometimes overwhelming. "Everyone's doing it!" you say. "It must not be so bad. Times have changed. It's not like that anymore," your heart says aloud.

Can I say? I never change. I AM the same yesterday, today and forever.

MY ways are higher than your ways. MY thoughts are above yours. MY heart does not change, and My love for you will not waver or subside.

Don't get caught up in the ways of this world, MY child. Don't allow the glitter and glam to pull you away for MY ways are full of excitement, overflowing. And MY Spirit is guiding you and teaching you the way.

Although it may seem hard to find in this clutter, just follow the steps one in front of the other. I promise it will lead you to great and mighty places, but if you get off course by cravings and deceptive ways, you will be downcast and afraid.

Hear ME child. Hear ME say it is by MY Spirit that I will guide you and show you the way. Don't get distracted by the ways of this world. Don't be fooled by all that you see. Just know and truly believe. My ways are higher and so much more for you to see!

Isaiah 55:8 (NLT)

"My thoughts are nothing like your thoughts," says the LORD.
"And my ways are far beyond anything you could imagine.

Hebrews 13:8

Jesus Christ is the same yesterday, today, and forever.

SO HOW BIG CAN U DREAM?

HOW big can you dream, MY child? How big can you dream? If it's not impossible, then it's not from ME.

I will show you ways that cannot be done without MY hand leading the way and shining the glory of the Mighty One.

So dream dreams bigger than the eye can see and believe. Nothing is ever impossible with ME.

Luke 1:37 (AMP)

For with God nothing is ever impossible and no word from God shall be without power or impossible of fulfillment.

DREAM BIG

What is the dream in your heart?
    Write the vision here and now.
Then run with it!

Habakkuk 2:2-3 (The Message)
And then GOD answered:
Write this.
Write what you see.
Write it out in big block letters
So that it can be read on the run.
This vision-message is a witness
    pointing to what's coming.
It aches for the coming—it can
    hardly wait!
And it doesn't lie.
If it seems slow in coming, wait.
It's on its way. It will come right
    on time.

_____
_____
_____
_____
_____
_____
_____
_____
_____
_____
_____
_____

Write it Out!

_____

_____

_____

_____

_____

_____

_____

_____

_____

_____

Be fearless.
Bold.
And strong.

WHO Я YOU?

>Be FEARLESS. BOLD. **AND STRONG.** <

Hang on to the pure, true and noble things and know where you belong.
I redeemed you out of darkness and into the light, upright and true.
I have made you MINE.
You are ROYALTY,

A MIGHTY WARRIOR &

Daughter Of The King.

. . . .

Philippians 4:8 (NLT)

And now, dear brothers and sisters, one final thing. Fix your thoughts on what
is true, and honorable, and right, and pure, and lovely, and admirable.
Think about things that are excellent and worthy of praise.

Ephesians 6:10

Finally, my brethren, be strong in the Lord and in the power of His might.

STAMP OF APPROVAL

Out of your heart flow the issues of life. Out of the abundance of your heart is where you will truly see what I have allowed to be planted there so deep no one is able to see.

Let MY Word, MY Spirit and MY mighty hand wipe away the hurt, the dirt from your small little hands.

MY daughter and MY beautiful saint, don't allow the world to put its brand upon you. Allow ME to show you a better way, a higher standard and a stamp of MY approval.

Listen, child! There is nothing in this world that can satisfy your soul. Nothing of this world can fill you full.

So don't allow the small things to interfere with MY plan. Learn to come to that quiet place that secret place with ME and wash away the untidiness and make you shiny clean.

I Love you. I LOVE YOU.

Proverbs 4:23

Keep your heart with all diligence, for out of it spring the issues of life.

Ephesians 1:13 (AMP)

In Him you also who have heard the Word of Truth, the glad tidings (Gospel) of your salvation, and have believed in and adhered to and relied on Him, were stamped with the seal of the long-promised Holy Spirit.

ONE OF A KIND

REDEEMED

- - - - - - - - - - - - - - - - - - - -

Cut these stamps out and leave them around your house. Let
them remind you of how God has put HIS stamps on your life.

Write it Out!

Make the room dark.
Light a flashlight or candle.
That's you!
Think about it.

"Let your light shine" (Matthew 5:16)

how bright can u b?

(Let) your light shine. Let your light shine bright for ME.

Don't allow the darkness all around to crush or smash it out.

MY light brings healing, joy and goodness to all who will step in.

MY light is for the world to see. MY light is for you to enjoy and help you become the woman I have created you to be.

You, My dear, are MY light in this world. You are the lamp lit brightly for those to see.

So don't hide away, but step out and shine because you're shining bright for ME.

Philippians 2:15 (NIV)

...So that you may become blameless and pure, "children of God without fault in a warped and crooked generation." Then you will shine among them like stars in the sky.

Matthew 5:14-15 (The Message)

"Here's another way to put it: You're here to be light, bringing out the God-colors in the world. God is not a secret to be kept. We're going public with this, as public as a city on a hill. If I make you light-bearers, you don't think I'm going to hide you under a bucket, do you? I'm putting you on a light stand. Now that I've put you there on a hilltop, on a light stand—shine!

TURN THE MUSIC UP –
WAY UP.
LOUDER
Than EVER before.
Dance
H–A–R–D–E–R
Than EVER
Before.

DANCE DANCE DANCE
DANCE DANCE
DANCE DANCE
DANCE DANCE

Dance a little jig

JUMPIN'! Dancin'! Spinnin'!

That is what you do when you're in MY presence and MY glory surrounds you.

Come. Dance before ME. Lift up your hands. And dance a little beat.

I AM joyful and fun, so bring yourself in this place and do a little jig.

Let us dance together—two by two. And let the laughter flow. Let it get all over you. My saints have become so stiff. They don't realize I made them to live joyful and fun with a spring in their step — never downcast, sorrowful and full of pity for themselves.

Come, MY child. Come dance a little dance. Lift up your hands. Give a little twirl, for I enjoy being with you. I have given you it all — joy, peace and abundance of ME.

So come and let your hair down. Come and dance with ME.

Ecclesiastics 3:4 (AMP)

A time to weep and a time to laugh, a time to mourn and a time to dance.

Jeremiah 31:13 (NLT)

The young women will dance for joy, and the men—old and young—will join in the celebration. I will turn their mourning into joy. I will comfort them and exchange their sorrow for rejoicing.

where

?

BU
E

Seriously, where do I fit?

You ask ME: | "God, where do I fit?"
"Where do I go from here?"
"What am I called to do, and where do my shoes fit?"

Sometimes you don't see everything up front. Sometimes I keep things hidden and reserved for a specific time and place, only to build you up.

When you trust ME each day for just the right amount of light, then you can follow close and we can keep in touch.

When you try to figure it all out yourself, then you fall into despair and become weary and feel like you just don't care.

So child, believe you have a perfect place in MY plan. Believe that the more you trust ME, the more light you will see.

Lift up your head. Be full of cheer, for the steps you are taking are mightier than you can dream and know you fit exactly where you're supposed to be.

I AM not early or late, for MY time is perfect. All you need to do is wait.

Psalm 119:105 (NLT)

Your word is a lamp to guide my feet and a light for my path.

2 Peter 3:9 (NIV)

The Lord is not slow in keeping his promise, as some understand slowness.
Instead he is patient with you, not wanting anyone to perish,
but everyone to come to repentance.

Talk Back!

_____

_____

_____

_____

_____

_____

_____

_____

_____

_____

_____

Wipe your eyes so you can see

Can you not see the path laid before you?

Can you not see MY hand holding you close and leading you on?

MY dear child, listen to the still small voice I have placed deep inside. Let it shout loud; let it be your guide.

There are many voices in this world, many sounds from every direction.

But MY children hear MY voice. They know when they sit quietly and learn My ways, then they will move out into the right path straight away.

Some may stumble and fall, many may lose hope and get caught in the ways of this world. But, I will always guide you in truth.

Although the road may not always be easy and pleasant, know that I AM leading you to places made specifically for you.

Walk close beside ME and hold out your hand for the plans I have for you are more than you could possibly think. They are beyond your wildest and most glorious dreams.

Listen closely today because there are many things I would like to say. Open your heart. Let yourself dream. And wipe your eyes clear so you are able to see.

John 10:4 (AMP)

When he has brought his own sheep outside, he walks on before them, and the sheep follow him because they know his voice.

Jeremiah 29:11 (NIV)

For I know the plans I have for you," declares the LORD, "plans to prosper you and not to harm you, plans to give you hope and a future.

You don't do GREAT things
when you hold back!

Full throttle

It is in that moment you hear a sound. You hear a sound from within—a voice speaking so loud. You hear, MY love. MY chosen one, do you know how awesome the road is that you're traveling on?

If you could only see up front—the blessings, the crowds, the royal hosts. Oh, what sights and joyful glee awaits. All you must do is believe.

The road has already been paved, marked out. It's showing the way. It only requires faith and a heart ready to go.

Come, child, it's time to hop on the road.

Look ahead through eyes of faith. Imagine an army in full guard leading the way.

No reason for fear. No shrinking back. Your steps strong and in full throttle.

Come on, MY girl, MY strong warrior. Be full of hope and remember ME saying, the road is marked, provided solid for you. All that's needed is your whole heart and bold attitude.

So know in this moment the plan is already made.

Be ready, and be on guard for your steps are paved.

Hear the voice saying, it's MY time now.

It's time to go forth. It's time to give a loud shout.

Luke 2:13

And suddenly there was with the angel a multitude of the heavenly host praising God....

Psalm 37:23 (AMP)

The steps of a [good] man are directed and established by the Lord when He delights in his way [and He busies Himself with his every step].

WHERE Я THE SIGNS, WONDERS & MIRACLES?

(Ever) wonder why this world has forgotten ME, MY signs, wonders and miracles?

Ever wonder why people decide not to believe anymore?

So many people tire themselves with the things of this world.

They choose to follow after idols, money and selfish desires. In doing so, they miss out of so much I have done for them.

But it's a new time. It's a new season for MY saints. MY power, MY Spirit is awakening this generation to a new level of worship, a new level of praise.

So before you decide to jump right in, Stop, look to ME. See for yourself the signs, wonders and miracles.

They are for those who decide to truly believe!

Hebrews 2:4 (AMP)

[Besides this evidence] it was also established and plainly endorsed by God, Who showed His approval of it by signs and wonders and various miraculous manifestations of [His] power....

Write down signs, wonders and miracles in your life and in others.

Encourage yourself in the Lord.

Be still. . . . Let God speak to your heart today!

your life is a blank canvas

When you give yourself to ME, I AM the artist, the designer who will make the masterpiece.

Stop looking at others and judging what you see.

Just stop and ask: God, what is in me?

Allow MY hand to paint the next scene and draw your life completely for ME.
Every piece different, all a perfect design for the glory of MY Spirit will be the center of your heart and the light that will shine.

So put away the thoughts of ME, standing at the door pointing MY finger and ready to scold.

No MY child, sit back and see. MY hand of perfection drawing out of you all the greatness that I have placed deep inside, for you are MY design, MY portrait, the glory of the Lord.

So stop looking at others, stop pointing things out. MY love is heavy and strong; you are MY design, made perfectly for ME.

So stop and smell the roses and allow ME to finish the painting one stroke at a time.
For I AM the Maker, the Master. YOU are the design.

1 Corinthians 11:31

For if we would judge ourselves, we would not be judged.

Isaiah 64:8

But now, O LORD,
You are our Father;
We are the clay, and You our potter;
And all we are the work of Your hand.

Write it Out!

YES YOU CAN

<u>**Yes**</u>, you can do all things through ME. Big things, small things, and things you never dreamed. You can see and do things beyond this world, just believe.

MY beautiful, precious daughter, you are who I adore; with ME living on the inside, you can do all things through ME.

So believe this, believe it with all your heart and watch your world open, expand and just step forth and start.

Know each step you take and everything you do; acknowledge ME and you will begin to accomplish everything with ME inside of you.

So know this with all your heart. You, MY child, can do all things--all things through Christ! Now all you need to do is start!

Philippians 4:13 (AMP)

I have strength for all things in Christ Who empowers me [I am ready for anything and equal to anything through Him Who infuses inner strength into me; I am self-sufficient in Christ's sufficiency].

Philippians 4:13

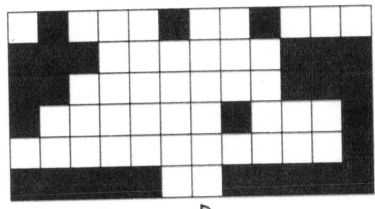

D

E H I E

C R N M N G W

R H N S U H E N O

S T H A R G T G S A S

I C T T I O T O H H L L

Write it Out!

_____

_____

_____

_____

_____

_____

_____

_____

_____

_____

Let's declare some things. In fact, tear out this page and put it on your mirror. Say these scriptures aloud daily and get God's Word off the page and working in your life.

I CAN

GOD in me is greater than he who is in the world.

If GOD be for me who can be against me?

GOD LOVES ME, AND HE HAS CALLED ME.

I am the righteousness of God through Christ Jesus.

no weapon formed against me can prosper.

I am strong in the Lord and the power of HIS might.

The SPIRIT OF GOD lives in me.

I'm anointed and well equipped, full of God's strength, passion and love.

i speak with authority, power, accuracy and knowledge.

I HAVE REVELATION AND KNOWLEDGE OF GOD'S WORD.

THE JOY OF THE LORD IS MY STRENGTH.

In HIS presence is the fullness of joy.

The peace of GOD reigns in MY heart.

If I keep my mind on GOD, I will have perfect peace.

GOD gives me peace that passes all understanding.

I HAVE POWER AND AUTHORITY OVER ALL THE WORKS OF THE ENEMY.

i am blessed, anointed, free and full of courage.

I am fearless and bold.

GOD has given me power, love and a sound mind.

I live by faith. I always win.

I can do all things through **CHRIST** who strengthens me.

Write your worries on this page.
Then tear it out and get rid of them.

Trust ME! Delight in ME.
And I'll take care of things.

NO GREATER DELIGHT

Delight yourself in ME and watch your day unfold.

Delight yourself in ME for weariness and demands
of life can take their bitter course.

Delight yourself in ME and hear your Savior say, "Your
heart's desires are secretly and quietly hidden away. I know
what you want. I know the very deep and hidden things."

So, MY dearly beloved, bring them to ME. For when you delight yourself in ME, then you will see those secret desires are MINE. I've placed so carefully.

Today I say, delight, MY child. Delight yourself in ME and watch your day unfold, and then you can truly see that MY greatest delight is you spending time away with ME.

Psalm 37:4 (AMP)

Delight yourself also in the Lord, and He will give you
the desires and secret petitions of your heart.

Sparkle

Sparkle and shine. Look bright as a brand new dime.

When people know you've spent time with ME, then they will see, the light bright and glory of ME.

Sing a song of praise. Just quickly lift up your voice and say: I am a child of the Most High God, crowned with jewels and ready to shine.

You don't need the sparkle of this world that burns out without the use of tools. No, MY child. You are the light of the world, a city on a hill, brightly shining for all to see.

So come and spend time with ME, and then the world will know I AM Jesus the Savior and all that's been told.

Sparkle and shine! Look bright as a brand new dime!

Matthew 5:14-16 (The Message)

"Here's another way to put it: You're here to be light, bringing out the God-colors in the world. God is not a secret to be kept. We're going public with this, as public as a city on a hill. If I make you light-bearers, you don't think I'm going to hide you under a bucket, do you? I'm putting you on a light stand. Now that I've put you there on a hilltop, on a light stand—shine!"

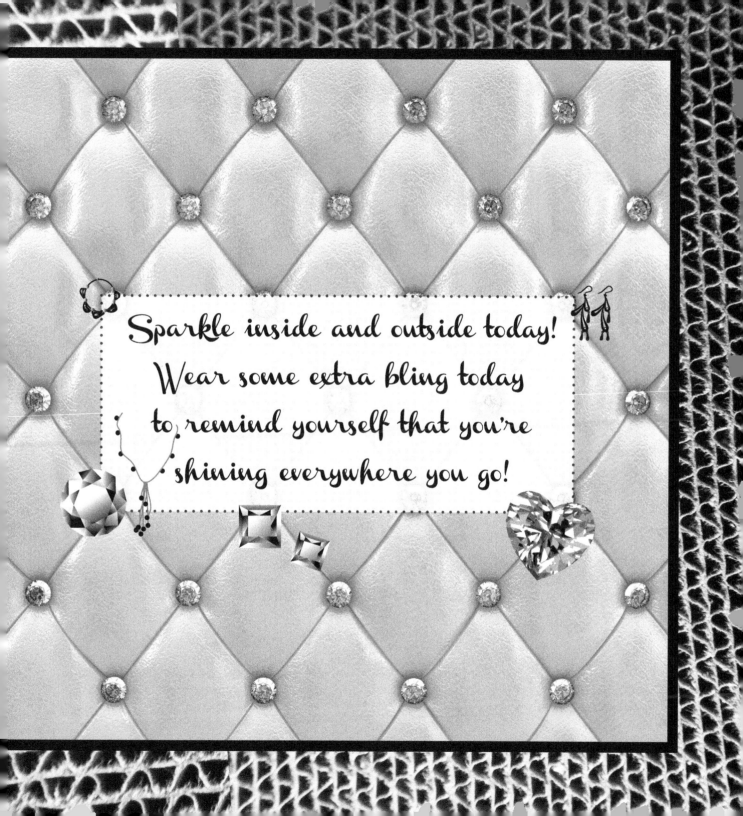

Sparkle inside and outside today! Wear some extra bling today to remind yourself that you're shining everywhere you go!

The best you

Child, don't get caught up in other people's lives. Don't compare yourself to their gifts and talents that you feel you don't have.

MY dear, you're the one I've called. So don't look at others but keep your focus clear and give ME your all. Then you will begin to hear.

Although you don't see every little detail, know and trust ME to see. Each piece of the design will fall in its place.

So stop looking at others in envy, stop thinking you're not enough. But put your trust in ME and be excited and full of hope. The path beneath your feet has been made smooth, paved for your feet to walk.

2 Corinthians 10:12 (NIV)

We do not dare to classify or compare ourselves with some who commend themselves. When they measure themselves by themselves and compare themselves with themselves, they are not wise.

Galatians 6:4-5 (The Message)

Make a careful exploration of who you are and the work you have been given, and then sink yourself into that. Don't be impressed with yourself. Don't compare yourself with others. Each of you must take responsibility for doing the creative best you can with your own life.

ill in the shapes with your special talents, callings and qualities!

What makes you YOU?

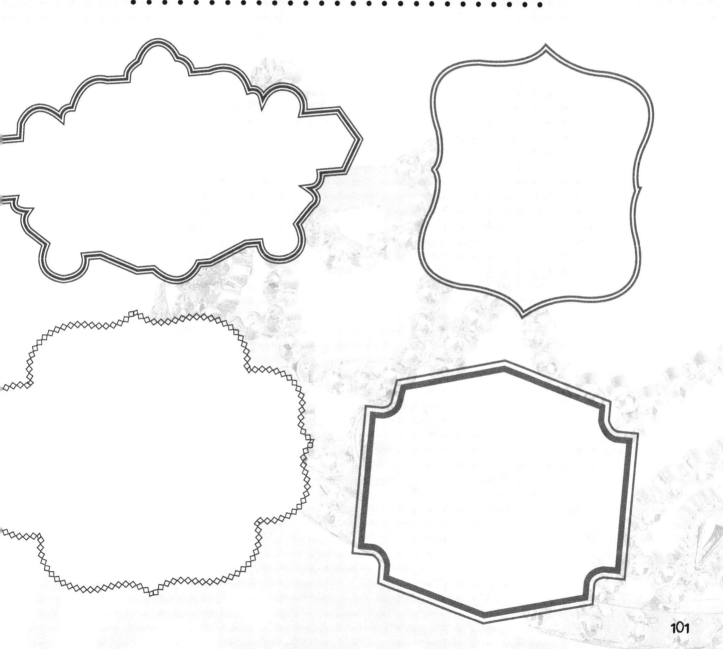

What adventures has God put in your life so far?
DO SOMETHING CRAZY WITH GOD TODAY!
TAKE HIM SOMEWHERE WILD!

Twists and turns

ENJOY. Enjoy. Enjoy. The journey with ME is full of joy. It's an adventure of a lifetime.

It's a life full of twists and turns and great things unseen. But when you come close beside ME then you will begin to see.

Come into MY presence. Come and see. Lift up your hands and just receive.

Hold on tight. Don't be afraid. The ride you are on will take you beyond what your eyes can see and your heart can dream.

It's MY turn, MY dear. It's MY turn to take hold, for on this adventure you will need a guide true and bold.

Come—enjoy. Enjoy and just be. MY great and mighty love for you will bring you face to face with ME and life beyond your wildest dreams. Enjoy. Enjoy. Just enjoy ME!

Hebrews 11:1 (NLT)

Faith is the confidence that what we hope for will actually happen; it gives us assurance about things we cannot see.

GIVE IT TO JESUS.

GET RID OF IT!

WORN OUT AND WEARY

Don't allow the weight of the world to bog you down. Lift up your face. Lift up your hands. I didn't come for you to be weary and worn out.

Bring all your burdens and all your cares to Me.

Cast them aside and learn to just be.

I AM here beside you, helping you through.

I will take the load and carry it for you.

I know in this world there seems to be so much stress, but you, MY child, need only to rest.

Rest in MY presence. Rest also in ME for I AM here comforting you and giving you MY peace.

Cast it all aside and come follow ME. Lay your weary head down. Lay down next to ME.

Matthew 11:28-30 (The Message)

"Are you tired? Worn out? Burned out on religion? Come to me. Get away with me and you'll recover your life. I'll show you how to take a real rest. Walk with me and work with me—watch how I do it. Learn the unforced rhythms of grace. I won't lay anything heavy or ill-fitting on you. Keep company with me and you'll learn to live freely and lightly."

1 Peter 5:7 (AMP)

Casting the whole of your care [all your anxieties, all your worries, all your concerns, once and for all] on Him, for He cares for you affectionately and cares about you watchfully.

Talk Back!

MIRROR MIRROR

When you look in the mirror, what do you see? A beauty or something different? How do you compare to those all around, good, bad, indifferent? Not sure how you really feel?

This is who I see -- a beauty, a daughter of royalty.

I see an individual I have created just for ME, a beautiful girl I adore.

I see a child of the Most High God, fully adorned with precious diamonds and beautiful jewels.

I see a princess, a warrior, a soldier for the Lord.

So look again. Now what do you see? A beautiful, precious gem, a piece of precious gold all unique in itself.

You are handpicked and one of a kind. You're not like anyone else, but perfect in design, a beautiful reflection of Me.

Oh how marvelous, how perfect you are to ME.

2 Corinthians 3:18

But we all, with unveiled face, beholding as in a mirror the glory of the Lord, are being transformed into the same image from glory to glory, just as by the Spirit of the Lord.

1 Peter 2:9

But you are a chosen generation, a royal priesthood, a holy nation, His own special people, that you may proclaim the praises of Him who called you out of darkness into His marvelous light.

The 2 Faces of You

The Lie

LOSER
UGLY
FAT
STUPID
REJECTED
DEPRESSED

I am
a child of the Most High God,
crowned with jewels and
ready to shine!

Who are you in Christ?

I am _____

I am _____

I am _____

I am _____

I am _____

I am _____

I am _____

I am _____

I am _____

I am _____

RUN REALLY FAST

Don't run from ME, but run to ME. Run in to MY arms opened wide.

I call you MINE, forgiven, safe and untouched.

Child, come running in to MY arms. Know you are safe within MY wings. It is here you can sit quietly and breathe easy with ME.

Don't hesitate. Don't fall back, but grab hold of MY hand and run really fast. There you will not lack!

Stay a while and rest, so when it's time to move out again, you will be full, clean and ready for anything.

So don't run away from ME. Come child. Run in to MY arms. Jump high. Run really fast!

Psalm 91:4 (AMP)

[Then] He will cover you with His pinions, and under His wings shall you trust and find refuge; His truth and His faithfulness are a shield and a buckler.

Who is He to you?

Get sticky notes.

Write different attributes of God, and post them all over your room as a reminder of just how great God is.

GOOD

FAITHFUL

HEALER

AWESOME

FRIEND

MIGHTY

Recall a time when your plans didn't go the way you thought they would, but ended up better than you expected.

YOUR PLAN	HIS PLAN

OFF COURSE

Some days don't **always** go **according** to your plans.

Sometimes I will take you off course in order to show something, speak something, or so you can do something for ME.

Don't be alarmed or even discouraged because this is a divine appointment, a meeting set up by Me.

When things fail to go as planned, just look to ME. Ask ME and watch ME take you places you've never been before.

Keep your eyes open. Keep your heart alert. And be ready for MY lead, ready for ME to take you off course.

Psalm 37:23-24 (NLT)

The LORD directs the steps of the godly. He delights in every detail of their lives. Though they stumble, they will never fall, for the LORD holds them by the hand.

Proverbs 16:9 (AMP)

A man's mind plans his way, but the Lord directs his steps and makes them sure.

FILL U UP!

It's in these quiet times I can speak clearly and directly to your heart. It's in these times when you wait on ME, I can pour MYSELF into you.

Life pulls, tugs and knocks you down. It drains all you have and tries to make you feel empty, inadequate and stressed.

Follow ME and life won't tear you down. Allow ME and MY ways to guide you. Remember I have given you an abundant life and carved a path through the crooked places and rough roads.

I didn't say life would be without trials, but with ME you can conquer it all.

Child, when you don't start your day with ME, your walk through life grows empty and afraid. So take a minute or two and sit quietly with ME. Allow ME to fill you full for the journey for today.

You're not alone, empty and afraid.

For I AM building you up strong and mighty for the King.

John 10:10 (NIV)

The thief comes only to steal
and kill and destroy;
I have come that they may
have life, and have it to the full.

Isaiah 40:3-5 (The Message)

Thunder in the desert! "Prepare for GOD's arrival!
Make the road straight and smooth, a highway fit for our God.
Fill in the valleys, level off the hills,
Smooth out the ruts, clear out the rocks.
Then GOD's bright glory will shine and everyone will see it.
Yes. Just as GOD has said."

Empty or Full?
That is the question.

Conduct an experiment. Make a point to yourself.
1. Get 2 glasses.
2. Fill one with water.
3. Leave the other empty.
4. Now take a drink out of both glasses.

Get the point?

It's a whole lot better drinking from a full glass, huh?! (Air isn't very satisfying!) In the same way, it's a whole lot better living life FULL of God.

What can you kiss & tell about God?

1. _____

2. _____

3. _____

Kiss & tell

Kiss and tell. Tell all those you know about ME. Let them know MY love runs deep. MY mercy has no end. Grace I give for all who will receive.

Go tell all who will hear that your God, whom you haven't seen, says, "Go, MY child! Go kiss and tell!"

1 Peter 1:8 (NIV)

Though you have not seen him, you love him; and even though you do not see him now, you believe in him and are filled with an inexpressible and glorious joy.

HOW GREAT HE IS

Greater is He that is in me than he who is in this world...

I AM greater than anything that tries to come against you in this world.

I AM the greater One on the inside of you.

You can conquer all when you are led by **MY** Spirit. You can win any battle you face when your heart connects to **MY** truth.

Child, **MY** Word is magnified. **MY** Word is sharper than any double-edged sword. Shout **MY** Word to your mountain, believing that **I AM** the greater One living inside of you.

You can speak to anything in **MY** name.

So believe in **ME**. Believe in **ME** as I believe in you. Believe you and I are one, and we can change the world one by one.

Grab hold, **MY** dear, for **I AM** the greater One who lives on the inside of you. **I AM** greater than anyone.

....

1 John 4:4 (NIV)

You, dear children, are from God and have overcome them, because the one who is in you is greater than the one who is in the world.

Hebrews 4:12 (AMP)

For the Word that God speaks is alive and full of power [making it active, operative, energizing, and effective]; it is sharper than any two-edged sword, penetrating to the dividing line of the breath of life (soul) and [the immortal] spirit, and of joints and marrow [of the deepest parts of our nature], exposing and sifting and analyzing and judging the very thoughts and purposes of the heart.

GET TO KNOW ME.
I LIVE INSIDE OF YOU.
—GOD

G
O
D

Talk Back!

_____

_____

_____

_____

_____

_____

_____

_____

_____

_____

Write a song!

Just a few lines will do!

Sing it to God! REJOICE!

STAY AS LONG AS YOU CAN

Worship – what a place to be, so deep in MY presence, standing so close to ME.

When you worship, that is where things change. Here in MY presence, the world fades away.

Daily, I say, come boldly in, come into MY holy place and stay as long as you can. For in this sanctuary of praise, MY love, MY grace and MY glory will change you, and you will walk away refreshed, made new and stronger than you ever knew.

So come in today. Worship ME. Lift up your hands to heaven and seek MY face. For in this place of worship, you are truly changed.

Psalm 66:4

All the earth shall worship You
And sing praises to You;
They shall sing praises to Your name.

Write it Out!

_____

_____

_____

_____

_____

_____

_____

_____

_____

_____

MAKE A DATE WITH JESUS!
CELEBRATE WHO HE IS AND
WHO YOU ARE IN HIM!

cELEBRATE!

It's a party.
You're invited. Come celebrate.

It's an exciting day! It's a day to celebrate, a day to rejoice in ME.

Today is a day to remember. It's a day you will not forget, for I have made it a day to step out.

Step out into the path I have placed before you. Step out and just rejoice, for MY hand is leading and guiding you and showing you MY love.

Enjoy this day. Enjoy the time spent with ME, and then your heart and your eyes will be opened wide to see.

Come and celebrate. Come and rejoice today with ME. Then you will know each day is like a party, celebrating who you are in ME.

Psalm 150:6

Let everything that has breath praise the Lord.

NO SECRET WHO I AM

It is no secret. I AM GOD.

There is no question that I made it all. High and lifted. Majestic and true. Yet the love I have runs deep, wide and full for you.

I do orchestrate the sun, the moon and the stars, and I know every strand of hair and every secret petition of your heart.

I AM the One True God, full of mercy and grace, with a tender heart wanting intimacy and praise.

I AM the God who says, "MY beautiful daughter, I adore you. I have called you MY own. I have placed you deep under MY arm. Righteous and holy you are, the daughter, the child of the Almighty God."

Exodus 3:14 (AMP)

AND God said to Moses, I AM WHO I AM and WHAT I AM and I WILL BE WHAT I WILL BE; and He said, You shall say this to the Israelite's; I AM has sent you!

Matthew 10:30 (NLT)

...The very hairs on your head are all numbered.

No secret who I AM

The Great I AM

King of Kings

Bright morning star

PRINCE OF PEACE

The Way

Author and Finisher

My Deliverer

MY Friend

The Light

Lord of Lords

Son of God

The Truth

Messiah

SON OF MAN

Lion of Judah

Wonderful, Counselor, Mighty God

LAMB OF GOD

Deliverer

Advocate

HOLY ONE

Daystar

JESUS

MY Redeemer

Just Worship

My Glory

Glory, honor and praise. Lift up holy hands.

Glory, honor and praise. For this is where you stand in MY holy place, worshipping ME and lifting your voice to heaven giving your all to ME.

Stand in MY courts. Give a loud shout. Dance in the Spirit. Come and lie down.

No matter what the cost. No matter what you do. Here in the place of worship is where you are clothed and made new.

Glory, honor and praise. This is what you do. Lift up your voice and worship two by two. Come into MY presence. Lay everything down.

Come and hear ME say that you, dear one, are MY true friend. I will sit beside you and hear the words you speak. I will listen intently to all that you say.

Don't be afraid or wander off too far. When you're out of MY presence, you enter in the dark.

Come worship ME. Come into MY presence and be all you're meant to be-- holy, righteous and made in the image of ME.

Come. Worship. Holy. Holy. Holy. Come worship ME.

Glory, honor and praise, for I AM worthy of it all.

Psalm 145:3 (The Message)

God is magnificent; he can never be praised enough. There are no boundaries to his greatness.

Revelation 4:11

"You are worthy, O Lord, To receive glory and honor and power; For You created all things, And by Your will they exist and were created."

Write it Out!

_____

_____

_____

_____

_____

_____

_____

_____

_____

_____

_____

PUT ON YOUR FULL ARMOR today

Helmet

Belt of Truth

Breastplate of Righteousness

Sword of the Spirit

Shield of Faith

Step into your feet of the

gospel of peace

And take the helmet of salvation,

and the sword of the Spirit, which

is the word of God.

EPH 6:13-1?

Dress to kill

Dress to kill, battle ready for anything.

Sword and shield, your helmet of salvation.

A soldier for the Lord your God, a warrior for the King!

Arm yourself. Dress like you're ready and equal to anything.

Sharpen your sword. Ready your feet for peace. The armor of the Lord is all you're going to need.

Dress yourself, MY child. Dress yourself today, for you never know what's in front and the battle you might face.

For the enemy will do all he can to try and trip you up today, but when you put your trust in ME and believe where you stand, know you are battled ready; dressed to kill and ready for anything.

Ephesians 6:13-17 (NIV)

Therefore put on the full armor of God, so that when the day of evil comes, you may be able to stand your ground, and after you have done everything, to stand. Stand firm then, with the belt of truth buckled around your waist, with the breastplate of righteousness in place, and with your feet fitted with the readiness that comes from the gospel of peace. In addition to all this, take up the shield of faith, with which you can extinguish all the flaming arrows of the evil one. Take the helmet of salvation and the sword of the Spirit, which is the word of God.

Philippians 4:13 (AMP)

I have strength for all things in Christ Who empowers me [I am ready for anything and equal to anything through Him Who infuses inner strength into me; I am self-sufficient in Christ's sufficiency].

Come on. Step out.

Step out—step out and then you can see, all that's in front of

you and be all you can be—strong, courageous, a warrior for ME.

Take up your sword and shield and remember who you are...

A mighty warrior for The Most High God!

Step out.

Ephesians 6:16-17

Above all, taking the shield of faith with which you will be
able to quench all the fiery darts of the wicked one. And take the helmet
of salvation, and the sword of the Spirit, which is the word of God.

Go read these words in your mirror. Then take a good long look at yourself. How can you step out?

Don't limit God.
Don't limit yourself.
Don't limit God in you!

SOUNDS OF PRAISE

Sing a song. Sing a song from your heart. Lift your voice to heaven and hook up with MY part.

Let your voice be heard.

Shout it from the mountain top.

Sing **a little song,** MY **daughter.**

Sing with all your heart.

Psalm 96:1

Oh, sing to the LORD a new song!
Sing to the LORD, all the earth.

Who I say you are

...by the blood of the Lamb and by the word of their testimony....
Revelation 12:11

Your sins are forgiven. They are washed away by the blood of the Lamb. Your sins are far from ME, says the Lord...as far as the east is from the west. I remember them no more.

I remember when you were born. I called you before you were even here on this earth. I called you with an everlasting love, and I put MY stamp of approval on you. You think because of all the mess you've made or the hurt you've been through that you're not worthy of MY love.

But that it so not true.

MY love for you runs too deep for you to even comprehend.

MY life was shed for you. MY blood has redeemed you from all sin and all the pain and hurt.

All you need to do is reach forth and receive.

You've been told you're unworthy, but I say YOU ARE REDEEMED.

You've been told your life is not worth anything, but **I SAY YOUR LIFE WAS WORTH DEATH FOR ME.**

Do not allow the enemy to lie to you any longer. Receive from ME. Receive MY love, MY power and MY Spirit. Allow ME to show you how to fight and win.

MY love for you is deep, and MY hope for you is BIG.
Come to ME and believe.

I AM calling you.

I have watched from afar.

Now I invite you. Come and follow ME.

Jesus

Now write your own story....
Has it changed?

Author Bio

Author and Bible college graduate Monica Withers is passionate about sharing the reality of an intimate relationship with Jesus Christ with young women and women young at heart.

Monica is all about empowering women to be all they can be. As a personal trainer and instructor for 30 years, Monica has devoted her professional life to helping women shape their bodies. Now she wants to help women connect to their real beauty as their relationship with God begins deep inside, but shows up outside revealing one-of-a-kind, unique, beautiful women.

Monica has been married to her best friend and partner, Mark, for more than 30 years. They make their home in Tulsa, Oklahoma.

Coming soon!

GODtalk
The Radical Side of Love

For more information about the God Talk series, new releases and more, check out www.**radicalgod.com.**

CPSIA information can be obtained at www.ICGtesting.com
Printed in the USA
LVOW02s2030160815

450208LV00006BD/7/P